BASKING SHARK

By Jennifer Boothroyd

Consultant: Erin McCombs
Educator, Aquarium of the Pacific

BEARPORT
PUBLISHING

Minneapolis, Minnesota

Credits

Cover and title page, © Charles Hood/Alamy, © sumroeng chinnapan/Shutterstock, © AP focus/Shutterstock; 3, © nabil refaat/Shutterstock; 4-5, © Chris Gomersall/Alamy; 5, © Maartje van Caspel/iStockPhoto; 6-7, © Martin Prochazkacz/Shutterstock; 8-9, © Charles Hood/Alamy; 9, © Napat/Shutterstock; 10-11, © George Karbus Photography/Getty; 12-13, © Howard Hall/BluepPlanetArchive; 13, © Charles Hood/Alamy; 14-15, © Dado Daniela/Getty; 16-17, © Pally/Alamy; 18, © Arsty/iStockPhoto; 18-19, © Gavin Parsons/Alamy; 19, © liveslow/iStockPhoto; 20-21, © Charles Hood /Alamy; 22, © Charles Hood/Alamy; 22-23, © nabil refaat/Shutterstock; 24, © nabil refaat/Shutterstock.

President: Jen Jenson
Director of Product Development: Spencer Brinker
Senior Editor: Allison Juda
Associate Editor: Charly Haley
Designer: Colin O'Dea

Library of Congress Cataloging-in-Publication Data

Names: Boothroyd, Jennifer, 1972- author.
Title: Basking shark / by Jennifer Boothroyd.
Description: Minneapolis, Minnesota : Bearport Publishing Company, [2022] |
   Series: Shark shock! | Includes bibliographical references and index.
Identifiers: LCCN 2021039169 (print) | LCCN 2021039170 (ebook) | ISBN
   9781636915289 (library binding) | ISBN 9781636915371 (paperback) | ISBN
   9781636915463 (ebook)
Subjects: LCSH: Basking shark--Juvenile literature.
Classification: LCC QL638.95.C37 B66 2022 (print) | LCC QL638.95.C37
   (ebook) | DDC 597.3--dc23
LC record available at https://lccn.loc.gov/2021039169
LC ebook record available at https://lccn.loc.gov/2021039170

For more information, write to Bearport Publishing, 5357 Penn Avenue South, Minneapolis, MN 55419.

CONTENTS

Is It a Sea Monster?

A dark blob moves slowly near the top of the water. What's hiding just below the ocean waves? Is it a sea monster? Nope! It's a basking shark. The tips of its fins and nose can be seen above the water. The shark is swimming with its mouth open, feasting on lots of tiny food.

Basking sharks may have **inspired** made-up stories about sea monsters from long ago.

A Mighty Big Fish

Beneath the water's **surface** is the basking shark's giant body. These animals are the second-biggest sharks in the world. Basking sharks can be up to 40 feet (11 m) long—about the size of a school bus!

The huge sharks have small eyes and long noses. They can't see well, but they have an excellent sense of smell.

Basking sharks are brownish gray.

Open Wide

The basking shark uses its sense of smell to find food. Its only **prey** are tiny plants and animals called **plankton**. The huge shark eats by opening its mouth about 3 ft (1 m) wide. As it swims, more than 100,000 gallons (379,000 L) of water rush into its mouth every hour, along with the plankton. That much water could fill a swimming pool!

Most plankton are smaller than grains of rice. Basking sharks need to eat millions of them a day.

ON THE MOVE FOR FOOD

Basking sharks swim and eat near **coasts** around the world. They stay in waters with **moderate** temperatures because their prey cannot live in places that are very cold or very warm. When the water temperature changes, the sharks **migrate** to follow their food.

BASKING SHARKS AROUND THE WORLD

Arctic Ocean

EUROPE

ASIA

NORTH
AMERICA

Atlantic
Ocean

AFRICA

Pacific
Ocean

Pacific
Ocean

SOUTH
AMERICA

Indian
Ocean

AUSTRALIA

N
W E
S

Southern Ocean

ANTARCTICA

Where basking sharks live

Basking sharks migrate alone, in pairs, or in large groups of more than 100.

What's Up With Gills?

As a basking shark swims, water flows into its mouth and **gills**. Parts of the gills collect plankton. Then, the shark closes its mouth to swallow the plankton.

A basking shark's gills also get **oxygen** from the water. This is how the shark breathes. After the shark gets oxygen, the water flows out of large gill slits on the shark's head.

The basking shark has some of the longest gill slits of any shark. The gills almost wrap around the shark's whole head.

Gill slits

Sharks in Danger!

Because basking sharks eat only plankton, they don't hunt for fish like many other sharks. And there aren't any ocean animals that hunt basking sharks, either. But these sharks are still in danger because of humans. People hunt basking sharks, which has led to fewer of these sharks in the world.

Basking sharks are also harmed when they are caught in nets intended for other fish.

Stop Bothering Me

While basking sharks don't have any ocean **predators**, they do have some animals bothering them. Tiny fish lice may attach themselves to basking sharks and feed on their skin. But there is another fish that helps the sharks. Pilot fish are small fish that sometimes swim alongside basking sharks. They eat lice off the sharks' bodies.

Basking shark skin is covered in sharp little scales called **denticles**.

Pilot fish

JUMPING SHARKS

Lampreys are another fish that hang on to basking sharks' skin. But basking sharks have a great way to get rid of these pests. The sharks jump into the air—as high as 4 ft (1.2 m) above the water! They swim straight up and out of the water with a burst of speed. This makes the lampreys let go.

Lamprey

The lamprey has a mouth full of teeth that it uses to hold on to basking sharks.

A Pup's Life

After growing inside their mothers for three years or more, baby basking sharks are born ready to jump, swim, and find plankton to eat. The **pups** are more than 5 ft (1.5 m) long when they are born. They grow bigger as they get older. When basking sharks are about 12 years old, they can have their own pups.

Scientists think basking sharks may live to be about 50 years old.

MORE ABOUT
BASKING SHARKS

Basking sharks never stop swimming. This keeps water flowing over their gills so they always have oxygen.

Basking sharks swim about 2 miles per hour (3.2 kph) while eating.

There are hundreds of tiny teeth in a basking shark's huge mouth.

Basking sharks have smaller brains than other sharks. Much of their brain power is used to smell for food.

Basking sharks weigh about 5 tons (4.5 metric tons). That's as heavy as an elephant!

Baby basking sharks' noses are curved up when they are born. But the noses straighten out as the pups get older.

GLOSSARY

coasts edges of land that touch an ocean

denticles small toothlike scales on sharks' skin

gills the body parts of water animals used for breathing

inspired gave someone an idea

migrate to move from one place to another

moderate in the middle; not too warm and not too cold

oxygen an invisible gas in air and water that animals need to live

plankton very small plants and animals that float in oceans

predators animals that hunt and kill other animals for food

prey animals that are eaten by other animals

pups baby sharks

surface the top of water

Index

Read More

Levy, Janey. *Sharks and Cleaner Fish (Animal Pals).* New York: Gareth Stevens Publishing, 2021.

Pettiford, Rebecca. *Basking Sharks (Blastoff! Readers: Shark Frenzy).* Minneapolis: Bellwether Media, 2021.

Learn More Online

1. Go to **www.factsurfer.com** or scan the QR code below.
2. Enter "**Basking Shark**" into the search box.
3. Click on the cover of this book to see a list of websites.

About the Author

Jennifer Boothroyd enjoys learning about basking sharks. They are one of her favorite animals, along with manatees and wombats.